The House of CHRISTMAS

GK Chesterton

Copyright © 2024. All Rights Reserved. Printed in the United States of America.

This book was produced by Libertas Kids, an imprint of Code Publishing, Covington, LA. LibertasKids.com
ISBN 978-1-60020-141-7 Ebook: 978-1-60020-142-4

There fared a mother driven forth
Out of an inn to roam;
In the place where she was homeless
All men are at home.
The crazy stable close at hand,
With shaking timber and shifting sand,
Grew a stronger thing to abide and stand
Than the square stones of Rome.

For men are homesick in their homes,
And strangers under the sun,
And they lay on their heads in a foreign land
Whenever the day is done.
Here we have battle and blazing eyes,
And chance and honour and high surprise,
But our homes are under miraculous skies
Where the yule tale was begun.

A Child in a foul stable,
Where the beasts feed and foam;
Only where He was homeless
Are you and I at home;
We have hands that fashion and heads that know,
But our hearts we lost - how long ago!
In a place no chart nor ship can show
Under the sky's dome.

This world is wild as an old wives' tale,
And strange the plain things are,
The earth is enough and the air is enough
For our wonder and our war;
But our rest is as far as the fire-drake swings
And our peace is put in impossible things
Where clashed and thundered unthinkable wings
Round an incredible star.

To an open house in the evening
Home shall men come,
To an older place than Eden
And a taller town than Rome.

To the end of the way of the wandering star,
To the things that cannot be and that are,
To the place where God was homeless
And all men are at home.

In the bleak midwinter, frosty wind made moan,
Earth stood hard as iron, water like a stone;
Snow had fallen, snow on snow, snow on snow,
In the bleak midwinter, long ago.

Our God, Heaven cannot hold Him, nor earth sustain;
Heaven and earth shall flee away when He comes to reign.
In the bleak midwinter a stable place sufficed
The Lord God Almighty, Jesus Christ.

Enough for Him, whom cherubim, worship night and day,
Breastful of milk, and a mangerful of hay;
Enough for Him, whom angels fall before,
The ox and ass and camel which adore.

Angels and archangels may have gathered there,
Cherubim and seraphim thronged the air;
But His mother only, in her maiden bliss,
Worshipped the beloved with a kiss.

Step softly, under snow or rain,
 To find the place where men can pray;
The way is all so very plain
 That we may lose the way.

Oh, we have learnt to peer and pore
 On tortured puzzles from our youth,
We know all the labyrinthine lore,
We are the three wise men of yore,
 And we know all things but truth.

We have gone round and round the hill
 And lost the wood among the trees,
And learnt long names for every ill,
And serve the made gods, naming still
 The furies the Eumenides.

The gods of violence took the veil
 Of vision and philosophy,
The Serpent that brought all men bale,
He bites his own accursed tail,
 And calls himself Eternity.

Go humbly ... it has hailed and snowed...
    With voices low and lanterns lit;
So very simple is the road,
    That we may stray from it.

The world grows terrible and white,
    And blinding white the breaking day;
We walk bewildered in the light,
For something is too large for sight,
    And something much too plain to say.

The Child that was ere worlds begun
    (... We need but walk a little way,
We need but see a latch undone...)
The Child that played with moon and sun
    Is playing with a little hay.

The house from which the heavens are fed,
    The old strange house that is our own,
Where trick of words are never said,
And Mercy is as plain as bread,
    And Honour is as hard as stone.

Go humbly, humble are the skies,
    And low and large and fierce the Star;
So very near the Manger lies
    That we may travel far.

Hark! Laughter like a lion wakes
    To roar to the resounding plain.
And the whole heaven shouts and shakes,
For God Himself is born again,
And we are little children walking
    Through the snow and rain.

www.ingramcontent.com/pod-product-compliance
Lightning Source LLC
Chambersburg PA
CBHW041603070526
44586CB00003BA/66